north west frontier province
(NWFP)

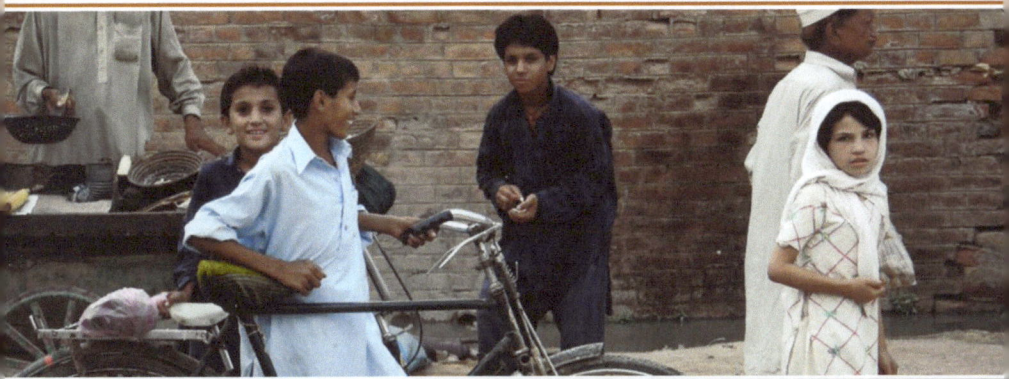

PROVINCIAL HANDBOOK / A Guide to the People and the Province

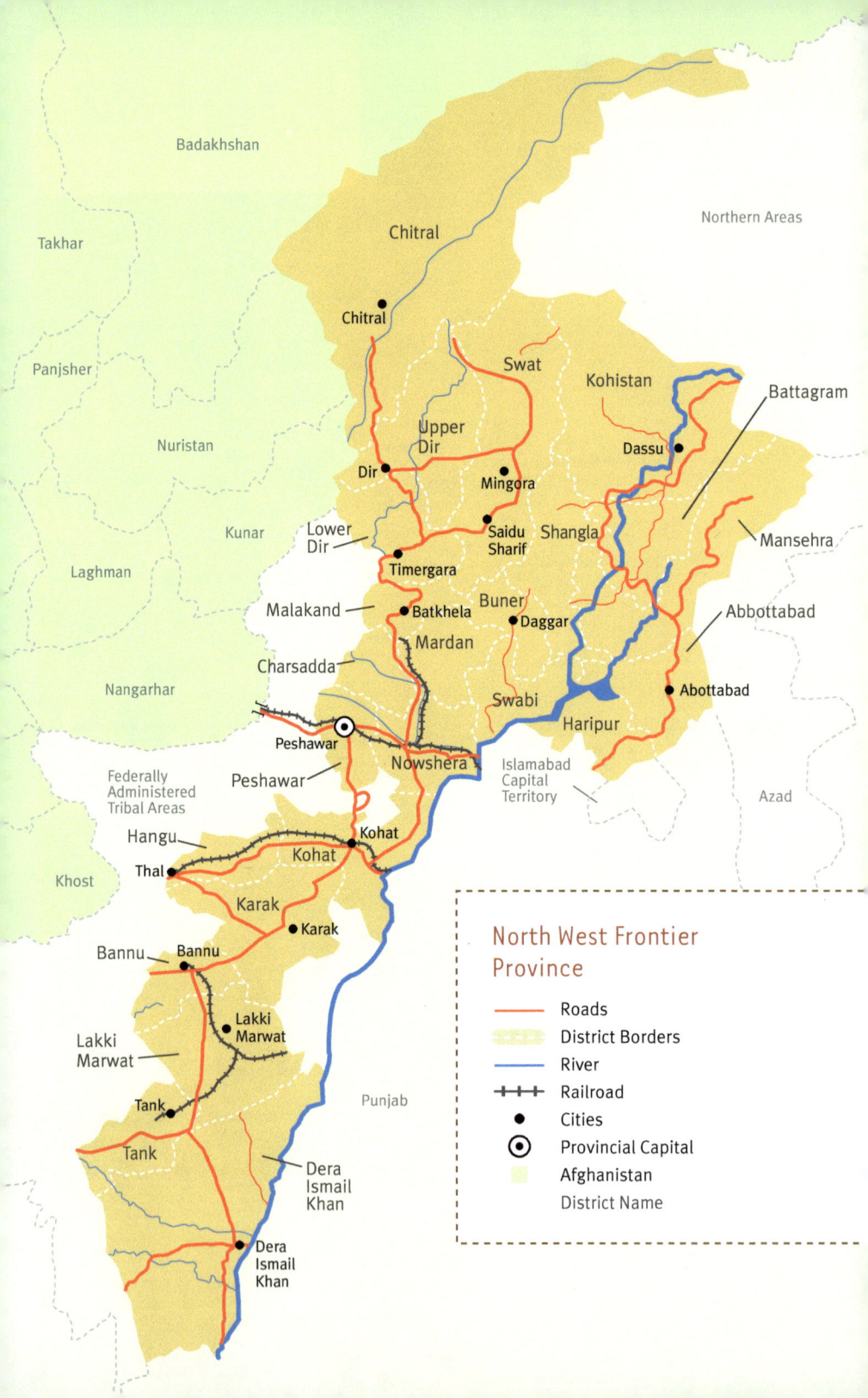

Badakhshan

Takhar

Panjsher

Nuristan

Kunar

Laghman

Nangarhar

Khost

Federally
Administered
Tribal Areas

Northern Areas

Chitral

Chitral

Swat

Kohistan

Battagram

Upper
Dir

Dir

Dassu

Mingora

Mansehra

Lower
Dir

Saidu
Sharif

Shangla

Timergara

Abbottabad

Malakand

Batkhela

Buner

Daggar

Abbottabad

Mardan

Charsadda

Swabi

Peshawar

Swabi

Haripur

Peshawar

Nowshera

Islamabad
Capital
Territory

Azad

Hangu

Kohat

Thal

Kohat

Karak

Karak

Bannu

Bannu

Lakki
Marwat

Lakki
Marwat

Tank

Tank

Punjab

Dera
Ismail
Khan

Dera
Ismail
Khan

North West Frontier
Province

Roads	
District Borders	
River	
Railroad	
●	Cities
◉	Provincial Capital
	Afghanistan
	District Name

Table of Contents

COVER: *Photo by Anthony Maw.*

List of Tables and Maps

LIST OF TABLES

LIST OF MAPS

Guide to the Handbook

This handbook is a concise field guide to the North West Frontier Province (NWFP) of Pakistan. Along with our companion handbook on the Federally Administered Tribal Areas (FATA), the handbook is intended to help orient and inform civilian and military personnel who are engaged in the Afghanistan-Pakistan region (AfPak).

Setting policy and managing field operations in Afghanistan and Pakistan requires understanding the human dynamics in the Pashtun border areas. FATA/NWFP is the hub for Taliban insurgent activity in both countries. Understanding the history, people, politics, and economics of FATA/NWFP and why it is a base for militant extremists will inform a counterinsurgency strategy in the border area and inform efforts to overcome militant influence across the region.

Civilians and military personnel in Afghanistan will better recognize how the security, political, and economic networks in FATA and NWFP influence and relate to the situation in the border provinces of Afghanistan. Readers will better appreciate and consider the strategic effects of operations on both sides of the border. When engaging Pashtun leaders in Afghanistan, readers will better recognize the nature and importance of interests and influence extending across the border to FATA and NWFP.

Policymakers and program managers engaged with Pakistan will better understand how the political, cultural, and economic dimensions of FATA/NWFP foster its militant character. As in any counterinsurgency campaign, separating the people from the insurgency depends as much on the political and economic activities as security operations. The handbook will help readers understand who and what matters within FATA/NWFP, political and economic conditions and issues that shape the environment in FATA/NWFP, and the how and why of influencing militancy in the border areas.

Sources and Data

Key sources for this guide include the government of the Islamic Republic of Pakistan, non-governmental organizations (NGOs), academic publications, and United States government (USG) publications. The book reflects information and perspectives from Pakistani and international experts who have spent significant time on the ground in and around NWFP.

The authors and editors of this handbook aim to present accurate and credible information. The region is in transition and difficult to access, so there are varying viewpoints about the "ground truth" in NWFP and adjoining areas. We present government data to inform and orient, but we do not endorse its accuracy. Different groups – religious, insurgent, militant, political, and governmental – are trying to secure and expand their influence in NWFP, and scenarios in various parts of NWFP are changing quickly. The handbook focuses on providing basic information and a knowledge base that can be built upon, using, among other things, the list of recommended references and internet sites listed in the Appendix.

Information in this book is unclassified. The views and opinions expressed in this booklet are those of the authors and in no way reflect the views of the United States government.

The Electronic Update

Look for electronic updates to this book at *www.idsinternational.net/ afpakbooks*. Updates will cover any new developments, issues, and leaders that have emerged after publication. They will also provide corrections and expanded content in key areas based on feedback from readers.

We hope the handbook will continue to be a valuable tool in thinking about the challenges in NWFP. If you have questions, comments, or feedback for future updates or editions, please email *afpakbooks@ idsinternational.net*.

ABOUT IDS INTERNATIONAL

Publisher of Afghanistan Provincial Handbook Series and the FATA/NWFP Pakistan Books

This book is a part of a series of handbooks on Afghanistan and Pakistan provinces and regions. Other titles include Ghazni, Helmand, Kandahar, Khost, Kunar, Laghman, Nangarhar, Nuristan, Paktika, and Paktya, as well as NWFP and FATA.

In addition to publishing these handbooks, IDS International provides training and support to government agencies in the areas of politics, economics, culture, stability operations, reconstruction, counterinsurgency, and interagency relations. In particular, IDS is a leading trainer of the US military in working with Provincial Reconstruction Teams (PRTs) in Iraq and Afghanistan. IDS offers its clients expertise and experience in non-lethal dimensions of counterinsurgency and interagency collaboration in complex operations. The writers and editors on this project offer a lifetime of experience working in these provinces and share a dedication to bringing peace and prosperity to the people of Afghanistan and Pakistan.

Author: Hasan Faqeer

Editors: Nick Dowling and Amy Frumin

Editorial Reviews: Imtiaz Ali, Peter Bergen, and Bob Grenier

Assistant Editors: Tom Viehe, Katie Stout, and Chris Hall

IDS INTERNATIONAL GOVERNMENT SERVICES

1916 Wilson Boulevard

Suite 302

Arlington, VA 22201

703-875-2212

www.idsinternational.net

afpakbooks@idsinternational.net

PUBLISHED: JUNE 2009

This and other AfPak handbooks may be bought in either digital or hard copy format. Samples are available upon request. IDS International provides analysis to government and private organizations in the areas of politics, economics, culture, stability operations, reconstruction, counterinsurgency and interagency relations. For inquiries, please email *afpakbooks@idsinternational.net* or call 703-875-2212.

The vast territory of NWFP includes rugged mountain ranges in the north, fertile plains in the central valley, and dry rocky areas in the south. Different peoples with different social networks will be found in each of these areas.

PHOTO BY BILL SPENSE

Chapter 1
Orientation and Overview

P akistan's North West Frontier Province (NWFP), or Pakhtunkhwa as many Pashtuns call it, is a land of picturesque valleys, rugged mountain ranges, and fertile plains. One end of the province is located at the strategic juncture surrounding the famous Khyber Pass, providing the country's primary link to Afghanistan. The other end touches the Northern Areas connecting Pakistan with China through the beautiful Karakoram highway. The historic Silk Road also passes through parts of the province, and the legacies of great Buddhist and Hindu kingdoms of the past are visible through many archeological sites in the area.

Though often hailed as the land of Pashtuns, NWFP is diverse in its culture, ethnic heritage, and traditions. The famous dance of the Kalash in Chitral district or Hindko language spoken in Abbottabad, Mansehra, and Haripur districts are as representative of the history of this province as the courageous and rebellious character of many of the Pashtun tribes that live here. The Pashtuns of the province make up 65-70 percent of the population. They are better educated and have better job opportunities than other ethnic groups, but growing urbanization is changing the dynamics of the area.

NWFP is adjacent and closely identified with the now-infamous Federally Administered Tribal Areas (FATA), but it is also different in many ways. Aside from the stark contrast in the political and administrative setup of the two areas, tribalism is less of a factor in NWFP than in FATA. NWFP is more mainstream, and progressive political forces have done well whenever democratic systems have been in place (roughly 30 years in the country's 62-year life). However, economic factors, political worldview, and religious identity bring NWFP and FATA closer to each other at various levels.

With rich natural resources, attractive tourist spots, and hardworking people, NWFP could have been a developed and economically self-sufficient province. Sadly that is not the case. Literacy is low, healthcare is scarce, and law enforcement capacity is poor. In addition, illegal trade, influential smuggling rackets, and inadequate infrastructure tarnish the economy of NWFP. Conflict and extremism, exacerbated by poor governance, have brought about the current struggle for control between Islamic militants and the Pakistani government. Various militant factions associated with the Taliban are gaining strength, though counteroffensives by the country's armed forces are challenging them in parts of NWFP (especially Swat, Buner, and Bannu districts). These media-savvy new radicals on the political and social horizon of NWFP have mushroomed in many parts of the province through threats, violence, and vigilantism.

In the political arena, the success of progressive political forces in the 2008 elections is interpreted as ordinary peoples' response to the five years of rule by an umbrella group of religious parties. The real test of the government is whether it can first halt and then potentially reverse the Talibanization trends through economic development, better governance, and improved law enforcement capacity.

ORIENTATION

NWFP lies in the northwest corner of Pakistan. Wedged at the foothills of the Hindu Kush, NWFP borders Afghanistan to the northwest, FATA to the west, the Northern Areas and Kashmir to the northeast, and Punjab to the east. As the province was made up of a majority of Pashtuns, Pakistan decided in 2008 to rename it *Pakhtunkhwa* ("land of the Pashtuns") despite objections from the non-Pashtun groups who constitute roughly 30 percent of the population. Divided into 24 administrative districts, the province covers an area of 75 sq km (29 square miles) and is home to an estimated 20 million people. While similar to FATA in its ethnic make-up, NWFP has been incorporated into Pakistan's governing structure as a province, with a political and administrative system in place – a primary reason for why it is often referred to as the "settled areas."

Geographically, the province is bisected by the Kabul River into two major zones. The northern zone is dominated by high mountains, extending from the slopes of the Hindu Kush to the borders of the Peshawar Basin. While warm during the summer, snowfall makes the northernmost areas of this zone inaccessible during the winter months. There are many tourist attractions in the northern zone, from the scenic lakes of Swat to the resorts of Nathiagalli in the east, although many of these areas have been disrupted by recent fighting. The Karakorum Highway follows the Indus River north, connecting Pakistan to China and functioning as the main source of trade for the eastern districts.

The southern zone stretches from Peshawar to the Derajat Basin. It is hot and humid in the summer and cold with scant rainfall in the winter. This zone is bordered by Punjab province to the east and FATA to the west, with many roads connecting the two. The Indus River, travelling along the eastern border, is the main source for irrigation, although this zone remains highly underdeveloped. Bannu district on the border with

FATA is home to many historical relics dating back to the 2nd century BC, such as the Akra mounds of the ancient Indus Valley Civilization.

Dividing these zones is the fertile valley of the Peshawar Basin, extending northward along the Kabul River. It is the home to about half of the province's total population, including its capital, Peshawar.

Unlike in many other parts of Pakistan (especially Punjab province), historic names of towns and districts derived from Hindu, Sikh, and other non-Islamic traditions are still popular in the province. For instance, Haripur is named after the Sikh general Hari who was governor of Kashmir in the early 19th century. Similarly, Lakki Marwat is named after its Hindu founder Lakki Ram or *Luko Ram-e Hind*.

Peshawar

The capital of NWFP and the district headquarters, Peshawar is the largest city of the province with over two million people. Deriving its name from the Sanskrit word *pushpapura* ("city of flowers"), it is about 40 kilometers from Afghanistan and is in essence a frontier town. Historically part of the Silk Road, Peshawar serves as headquarters for the Frontier Corps (FC), the paramilitary force operating in both FATA and NWFP.

Table 1: District Populations

DISTRICT	CAPITAL	POPULATION	TRIBES AND ETHNICITIES
Abbottabad	Abbottabad	880,666	Abbassis and Jadoons
Bannu	Bannu	675,667	Bannuchi and Jadoons
Battagram	Battagram	307,278	Gujar, Swati, Akunkhel, and Medakhel
Buner	Daggar	506,048	Yousafzai and Mandani Yousafzai
Charsadda	Charsadda	1,022,364	Mohammadzai, Mohmand, and Gigiani
Chitral	Chitral Town	318,689	Khow, Adamzada, Arbabzada, Kalash, Palula, Dameli, Nuristani, Burushaski, Wakhi, Kyrgyz, and Persian
Dera Ismail Khan	Dera Ismail Khan	852,995	Baloch, Muhajirs, Jat, and Pashtuns (Mottani tribe)
Hangu	Hangu	314,529	Bangash, Orakzai, Khattak, Shinwari, and Afridi
Haripur	Haripur	692,228	Jadoon, Tareen, Dilazaq, Tanolis, Sardar, Awan, and Rajas
Karak	Karak	130,796	Khatak
Kohat	Kohat	562,644	Bangash and Khatak

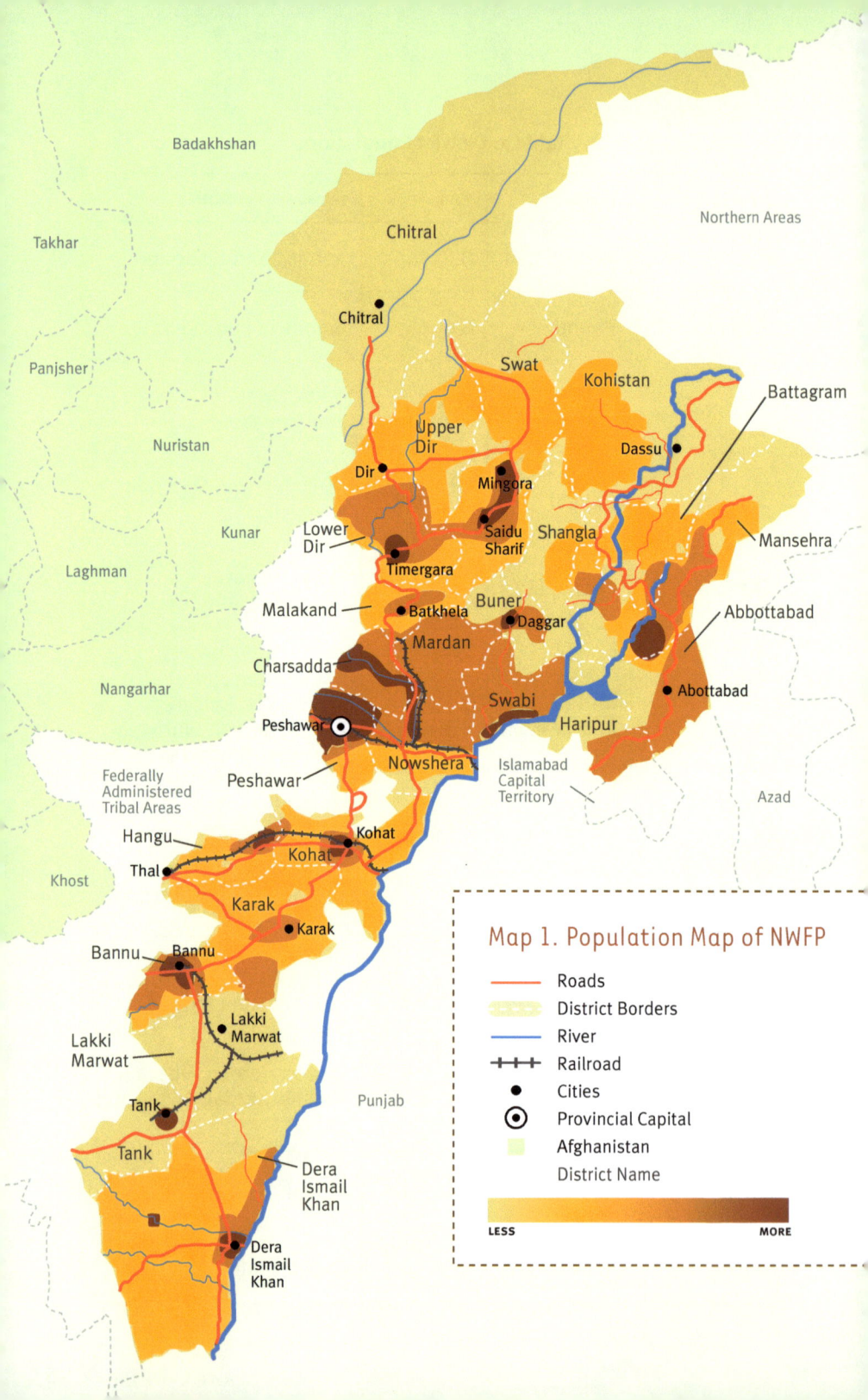

Map 1. Population Map of NWFP

Legend:
- Roads
- District Borders
- River
- Railroad
- Cities
- Provincial Capital
- Afghanistan
- District Name

LESS — MORE

Districts and cities:
- Badakhshan
- Takhar
- Panjsher
- Nuristan
- Kunar
- Laghman
- Nangarhar
- Khost
- Chitral / Chitral
- Swat
- Kohistan
- Dassu
- Battagram
- Upper Dir
- Dir
- Mingora
- Mansehra
- Lower Dir
- Saidu Sharif
- Shangla
- Timergara
- Malakand
- Batkhela
- Buner
- Daggar
- Abbottabad
- Mardan
- Abbottabad
- Charsadda
- Swabi
- Peshawar
- Haripur
- Peshawar
- Nowshera
- Islamabad Capital Territory
- Azad
- Federally Administered Tribal Areas
- Hangu
- Kohat
- Kohat
- Thal
- Karak
- Karak
- Bannu
- Bannu
- Lakki Marwat
- Lakki Marwat
- Tank
- Tank
- Punjab
- Dera Ismail Khan
- Dera Ismail Khan

DISTRICT	CAPITAL	POPULATION	TRIBES AND ETHNICITIES
Kohistan	Dassu	472,570	Kohistani (Manzar, Money, Koka, Mankekhel, and Darramkhel)
Lakki Marwat	Lakki Marwat Town	490,025	Marwat
Lower Dir	Timergara	717,649	Mashwani, Shinwari, Yousafzai, Shahkhel, Mastkkhel, Umerkhel, Dushkhel, Mayar, Anikhel, Sultankhel, and Aka Khel
Malakand	Batkhela	452,291	Akozai, Yousafzais, and Uthmankhel
Mansehra	Mansehra	1,152,839	Mansehra
Mardan	Mardan	1,460,100	Yousafzai, Khatak, and Mohmand
Nowshera	Nowshera	874,373	Khatak
Peshawar	Peshawar	2,019,118	Afridi, Khatak, Orakzai, Wazir, Mehsud, Mohmand, Daudzai, and Chamkani
Shangla	Alpurai	434,563	Yousafzai
Swabi	Swabi	1,026,804	Yousafzai
Swat	Saidu Sharif	1,257,602	Yousafzai
Tank	Tank	238,216	Bhittani, Kundi, Kattikhel, and Marwat
Upper Dir	Upper Dir	575,858	Kohistani, Yousafzai, Katami, Roghani, and Swati

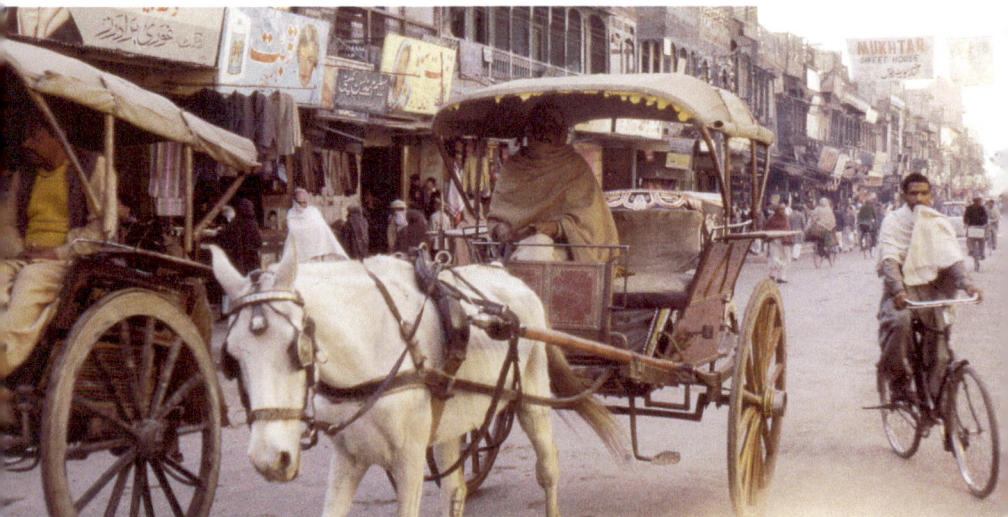

Peshawar has seen many conquerors throughout its history, including Genghis Khan, Tamerlane, and the British Empire. Each has left a mark on its culture, society, and politics.

PHOTO BY BILL SPENSE

Chapter 2
Relevant History

NWFP is the historic gateway to South Asia. The multitude of invading armies and passing empires have had a cultural, social, and political impact on the region, notably in the spread of Islam. However, NWFP has maintained its tribal ethos throughout history. The Soviet-Afghan War of the 1980s and the subsequent expansion of radical Islamist educational and political movements led to the current struggle where Taliban in the tribal areas threaten governments in both Pakistan and Afghanistan.

FROM ANCIENT TO MODERN TIMES

The area now called NWFP was once the heart of the ancient Gandhara Kingdom under Buddhist rulers (also known as Kushan kings) that thrived in the eastern Afghanistan and northern Pakistan from the 1st to 5th centuries. The blossoming of the Gandhara kingdom led to the spread of the Buddhist art and doctrines into the larger Asian continent. Later inhabitants also left a rich legacy, though less tangible but equally famous. The Gandhara kingdom was annexed by the Persian Achaemenid Empire in the early 6th century and the region then passed successively under Greek, Indian, and Mughal rule. Specifically, Peshawar remained an important province of Alexander the Great's dominion, as well as that of the Kushan Empire.

Islam first appeared in the region in the 8th century, when Arab fighters clashed with the Chinese near Chitral. However, Islam did not find a firm foothold in the region until the Afghans started empire-building in the 11th century. Beginning in the late 12th century, the region was held successively by various Muslim Afghan dynasties. Genghis Khan also stormed through Peshawar in 1221, with Tamerlane (Timur) following his footsteps at the end of the 14th century. Virtually all conquerors found the Pashtuns to be unruly subjects. By 1818, invading Indian Sikhs secured control of the frontier territory and maintained it for around three decades, though not without fighting Pashtun tribes in a series of battles (the most famous of which is the Battle of Balakot in 1831). Two rebel leaders whose strategy and conservative religious orientation is linked to today's militancy were Syed Ahmad Shaheed and Shah Ismail Shaheed.

THE BRITISH ERA

The Pashtun territories were a part of the British-controlled Punjab until Lord Curzon created NWFP in 1901. Due to the troubles in neighboring FATA in the 1870s, the British introduced the Frontier Crimes Regulations (FCR), prescribing special procedures for the tribal areas. The Pashtun tribes of FATA and NWFP, known for resisting history's most famous conquerors, earned the respect of the British. British policy aimed at subduing the tribes on their "northwest frontier" and keeping Russian influence at bay. In 1893, the British and Afghanistan negotiated a border – the Durand Line – dividing various Pashtun tribes between Afghanistan and British India, with FATA serving as a buffer zone.

One NWFP Pashtun leader, Bacha Khan, was a close associate of and fellow advocate for non-violence, along with India's renowned leader Mohandas Gandhi. Khan's leadership earned him the nickname "Frontier Gandhi." After Pakistan's independence in 1947, a referendum determined that NWFP would become part of Pakistan. NWFP remained strategically critical for Pakistan, given tensions between Pakistan and Afghanistan over territorial claims along the borders and the battle for mutual influence in each country.

SOVIET-AFGHAN WAR AND THE RISE OF THE TALIBAN

After the Soviet invasion of Afghanistan in 1979, the Afghan resistance launched from Pakistan's border areas. FATA served as the base camp and parts of NWFP, especially Peshawar District, provided the logistics back-up. Many NWFP districts, including those bordering FATA (especially Dir, Dera Ismail Khan, Charsadda, Kohat, and Bannu), became part of the supply line for supporting Afghan and Arab fighters. Religious radicals from many Muslim states around the globe were invited to fight the "infidel" Soviets. Most "reported for duty" in Peshawar, where many radicals and militants like Abdullah Azzam and Osama bin Laden set up their offices to make necessary arrangements for the training of these mujahedin. Pakistan's military and intelligence agencies spearheaded this effort on the ground and the US and some European states provided weapons and financial support for the project. Financial support from Saudi Arabia and Gulf countries was also important.

A *madrassa* (seminary) network emerged in NWFP to cater to the education and religious needs of the roughly three million Afghan refugees that poured into the region between 1979 and 1992. The madrassas helped spread the Saudi Wahhabist view of Islam and promoted the growth of religious conservatism generally. This education in an extreme form of Islam also fed into jihadist attitudes supporting the war in Afghanistan in dangerous religious terms.

After the Soviet withdrawal from Afghanistan, the extremist linkages and networks in the region strengthened further and many students of madrassas became known as the Taliban and moved from NWFP to Afghanistan to take part in the civil war for control of the country. The political rise of the Taliban in 1994-95 with official Pakistani facilitation also further empowered Pashtun tribesmen of FATA and NWFP who had played a role in the Afghan Jihad.

CONTEMPORARY DEVELOPMENTS

After US and Northern Alliance forces ousted the Taliban after the 9/11 attacks, many Taliban and foreign fighters fled to FATA and various parts of NWFP (especially in the districts bordering FATA).

The 2002 national and provincial elections marked the emergence of *Muttihada Majlis-e Amal* (MMA – United Action Forum), an umbrella group of six major religious political parties of the country. This alliance of conservative religious parties led by clerics was able to form a government in NWFP and became a powerful opposition block in the central legislature in Islamabad. The MMA government (2002-07) disappointed even its own supporters due to its corruption, nepotism, and incompetence. MMA rule seriously undermined civil liberties, legal reforms, and religious tolerance in the province. The MMA banned music, tried to further "Islamize" public education, and passed legislation amounting to sharia law. Despite major objections by opposition parties and even by President Musharraf, government of NWFP went ahead with the project. But Musharraf was not always anti-MMA. He overlooked some of the MMA's excesses, as he needed the MMA's support in the national legislature for constitutional amendments sanctioning Musharraf's role as army chief. It was this behind-the-scene collaboration that inspired critics to nickname the MMA government a "Mullah-Military Alliance."

The NWFP public rejected the MMA's conservative ways with the 2008 election victory of two progressive parties: Awami National Party (ANP) and Pakistan People's Party (PPP). ANP and PPP easily formed a coalition government in March 2008. However, the MMA's five years in government institutionalized a degree of Islamic radicalization in NWFP that remains in place today, including bureaucrats with radical religious views and conservative polices.

In 2008 and 2009, the rise of militancy in FATA and NWFP culminated in Taliban offensives in Swat and Buner. The increased violence and expansion of militant activity triggered a counteroffensive by Pakistani secuirty services. For more on these contemporary security developments, see Chapter 7.

NWFP is an ethnically diverse province made up of Pashtuns, Hindkowans, Kalasha, and Saraikis. Similarly, there are many languages and dialects spoken, including Urdu, Pashto, Hindko, Saraiki, and Baluchi.

PHOTO BY ANTHONY MAW

Chapter 3
Ethnicity, Tribes, Languages and Religion

ETHNICITY

NWFP is an ethnically diverse province. Pashtuns represent the largest ethnic group in the province, forming about two-thirds of the total population. They live in the western and southern parts of the province, including the capital, Peshawar. The majority of the remaining non-Pashtun population is Hindkowan, mostly living in the eastern districts of Haripur, Abottabad, and Mansehra. The Dardic people, such as the Kowar, Kohistani, Shina, Torwali, Kalasha, and Kalami, represent a minority, dominant in the northern districts of Chitral and Kohistan.

LANGUAGE

Three main languages are spoken in NWFP. Pashto is the most pervasive language in NWFP, spoken by nearly 70 percent of the people. Hindko, the Punjabi dialect of the Hindkowans, is spoken by roughly 20 percent of the population. Bilingualism is common among Pashto and Hindko speakers. Saraiki is spoken in the southeast of NWFP, mainly in Dera Ismail Khan district, by about four percent of the people.

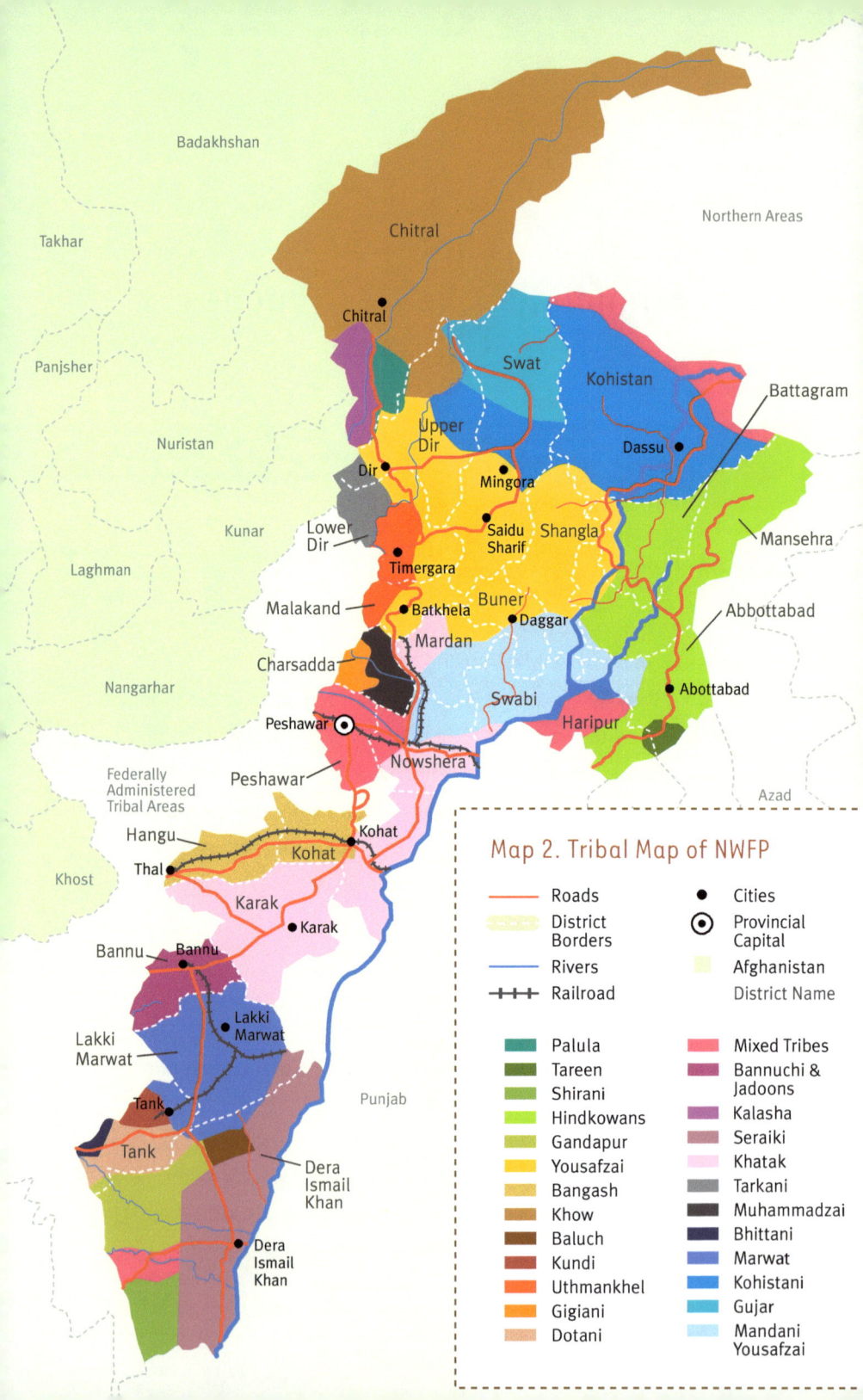

Map 2. Tribal Map of NWFP

Badakhshan

Takhar

Panjsher

Nuristan

Kunar

Laghman

Nangarhar

Khost

Chitral

● Chitral

Swat

Kohistan

Battagram

Dassu ●

Mansehra

Upper Dir

Dir ●

● Mingora

Lower Dir

● Saidu Sharif

Shangla

Abbottabad

Timergara ●

Malakand

● Batkhela

Buner

Daggar ●

Mardan

● Abottabad

Charsadda

Swabi

Peshawar ◉

Swabi

Haripur

Nowshera

Azad

Peshawar

Federally Administered Tribal Areas

Hangu

Kohat

Kohat

Thal ●

Karak

Punjab

● Karak

Bannu

● Bannu

Lakki Marwat

● Lakki Marwat

Tank

● Tank

Dera Ismail Khan

● Dera Ismail Khan

Northern Areas

Legend

Roads	Cities
District Borders	Provincial Capital
Rivers	Afghanistan
Railroad	District Name

- Palula
- Tareen
- Shirani
- Hindkowans
- Gandapur
- Yousafzai
- Bangash
- Khow
- Baluch
- Kundi
- Uthmankhel
- Gigiani
- Dotani
- Mixed Tribes
- Bannuchi & Jadoons
- Kalasha
- Seraiki
- Khatak
- Tarkani
- Muhammadzai
- Bhittani
- Marwat
- Kohistani
- Gujar
- Mandani Yousafzai

Urdu is also spoken by many in the province, though mostly as a second language, as it is Pakistan's national language and taught by all educational institutions. Baluchi is spoken in some villages of Dera Ismail Khan bordering Baluchistan province.

TRIBES

Pashtuns can be divided into four major branches: Sarbani, Batani, Ghorghashti, and Karlani. Within these are roughly 60 major tribes and over 300 sub-tribes or clans. The major Pashtun tribes living in NWFP include Yousafzai, Tanoli, Khatak, Marwat, Afridi, Shinwari, Orakzai, Bangash, Mehsud, Mohmand, Wazir, Swati, and Gandapur, as well as numerous other smaller clans. Important non-Pashtun tribes (mostly Hindkowans) include Awan, Syeds, Gujar, Tareen, Jadoon, and Mashwani. In addition, Afghan refugees, including Pashtuns from the Ghilzai and Durrani tribes, the Persian-speaking Tajiks, and some Hazaras, have settled around Peshawar. Many of these tribes compete in their local environs for political power and natural resources, such as the Mehsuds and Wazirs in Tank.

Unlike the adjacent FATA, tribal identity is less important and influential in the politics and society of NWFP. Indeed, there are fewer tribal rivalries, as most tribes are dispersed across different districts. Urban, rural, and class identities are comparatively more instrumental in defining the social, political, and economic outlook of the people. However, religious and sectarian affinities and networking are increasingly more relevant in NWFP today.

Yousafzais are primarily known for their class distinctions of khans (land holders) and peasants/landless farmers and for their internal rivalries. They are also remembered for the battles they fought against the Mughal and Sikh rulers in the 17th and 18th centuries. The most prominent sub-tribes are: the **Mandani**, who reside in Swabi and Mardan districts; the **Akozai**, who occupy the Panjkora and Swat valleys; and the **Iliaszai**, who live in Buner district. Yousafzais (literally meaning "sons of Joseph") originally migrated to present day NWFP in the fifteenth century, occupying Swat, Dir, Shangla, Swabi, and Mardan districts. Some even debate whether they were originally among the ten lost tribes of the Israel.

Among the Pashtuns, **Khattaks** are known for their endurance and perseverance. They traditionally have a higher literacy rate than most tribes in NWFP, with their most famous member, Khushal Khan Khattak (1613-1690), widely known for his inspirational poetry, which is still taught today in schools around Pakistan. Khattaks have strong clan loyalty and are divided into two major groups: the **Akora** and the **Teri**. One of the sub-tribes, **Khan Khel**, historically produced most of the tribal chiefs, while another sub-tribe, **Fakir Khel**, gained renown for producing many leading religious figures. Mostly residing in Kohat, Nowshera, and Karak districts, a few thousand **Khattak** tribesmen also live in North Waziristan, linking it to FATA.

Marwats are renowned as fighters. Seen as a warrior tribe, locals say they fought 60 battles. Residing in Lakki Marwat and Tank districts, Marwats originally lived in Paktya province in Afghanistan, but came to the area over time – often pushing their way in during times of conflict. This history soured relations with many neighboring tribes. They are one of the few tribes that still carry a tribal flag. It contains two golden crosses that are seen as symbols of their values: self reliance and self-defense. Physically, they are known for their strong and sturdy features and a fair complexion for Pashtuns.

Bhittanis are known as hereditary enemies of the Mehsud, who mostly live in FATA. Despite this rivalry, they have supported each other against anyone seen as an invader to the region, especially the British.

Bhittanis also have cool relations with Marwats, who often accuse the Bhittanis of stealing their land, highway robbery, and kidnapping. Living between Waziristan in FATA and Dera Ismail Khan district, significant numbers of Bhittanis also reside in Bannu district.

Among the non-Pashtun tribes of the province, the **Kalasha** of Chitral are the most unique. Seen as primitive, they are locally known as "Infidel Wearers of the Black Robe" since they are not Muslim, and "Kalash" also means black. However, the tribe is known for its colorful dress and exotic dance that is a source of major attraction for tourists. The tribe is peaceful, avoiding confrontation even when provoked.

Hindkowans are not organized by tribe. Also called Punjabi-Pashtuns because of their Punjabi dialect, they are believed to have mixed Arab and Pashtun/Afghan origins. However, their ethos and values are quite different from tribal Pashtun culture. While historically involved in local conflicts, their tradition does not cherish violence. Many are bilingual – fluent in both Hindko and Pashto.

Pashtunwali

Pashtun society is structured around a code of ethics known as *pashtunwali*, an ancient and chivalrous code of honor. In essence, it is a social, cultural, and quasi-legal code. It is unwritten, and no one individual, group, or publication is the source of this set of rules. For Pashtuns, it is the collective wisdom of their forefathers, a set of principles guiding both individual and communal conduct. It has varied sources, ranging from Sufi poetry, folklore of epic romances (such as Adam Khan and Durkhaney; Yusuf Khan and Shehrbano), and various *mataloona* (proverbs). It evolved over a period of centuries and some of its notions are mere clichés. The major components of pashtunwali are:

Melmastia (Hospitality): Pashtuns are known for their hospitality and will go to great lengths to treat their guests with honor and respect, regardless of race, religion, national affiliation, or economic status. This hospitality is conducted without any hope of remuneration or favor. Historically, even enemies were provided this privilege if they came to one's house.

Nang (Honor): All Pashtuns are required to safeguard the honor of the family in terms of independence, culture, and religion. This can be interpreted widely or narrowly depending upon the education and exposure of a person. Honor is also maintained by following the code of pashtunwali.

Badal (Revenge): Pashtuns are quick to take revenge for an insult or seek justice for a past crime. It does not matter if the insult is decades old. The only way to restore honor to the family, clan, or tribe is to exact revenge on the offending family, clan, or tribe.

Nanawati (Asylum): Pashtuns will provide protection to anyone who requests it against their enemies. Such a person is protected at all costs and under any circumstances.

Zemaka (Land/Earth): Pashtuns are required to defend their land and property from incursions.

Torah (Courage): Pashtuns have a tradition of bravery and courage in the face of a challenge.

Hujra (Sitting Place): Pashtuns typically provide a meeting place or assembly hall where any member of the community can come and discuss cultural or political issues. It also acts as a forum for conflict resolution and negotiation. The host of the *hujra* has specific responsibilities, especially regarding the safety of all visitors.

Among the many other features of Pashtunwali, the strongest are an abhorrence to accept outside interference in internal matters, disdain and reluctance to be governed by a distant "central authority," and an amazing confidence in the ability of local leaders to provide protection and an environment in which they can live according to their own traditions and practices. While Pashtunwali existed before Islam came to the region, they have since added some aspects of the Islamic law, sharia. According to critics, only such religious notions that conformed well with pashtunwali were willingly adopted.

RELIGION

Sunni Muslims make up the majority of inhabitants at 80 percent, with roughly 15 percent Shia (most being of the Isna Ashari sect). Like neighboring Kurram and Orakzai agencies, Shia-Sunni clashes are routine in Hangu district. In southern Chitral, the Kalasha maintain their ancient animist/shamanist religion. A small percentage of Hindus, Sikhs, and Christians also reside throughout the province. The Ahmadiyya, a minority Muslim sect that was controversially declared to be non-Muslim by Pakistan's Parliament in 1974, is also present.

A fortified tribal leader's home. While not as important to local governance as in FATA, tribes still play a very important role, especially in rural settings. An endorsement from the Marwat tribe, for instance, is necessary to win any election in their territory.

PHOTO BY ANTHONY MAW

Chapter 4
Government and Leadership

STRUCTURE OF THE GOVERNMENT

The 1973 Constitution of Pakistan set up a parliamentary system at both the national and provincial levels of government. Within this system, the Provincial Assembly selects a chief minister who forms a cabinet of ministers to look after various departments. Meanwhile, the president of Pakistan appoints the provincial governor after consulting the prime minister and provincial council. The real power lies with the chief minister, the provincial equivalent to the prime minister, who is the head of the executive branch. For most provinces, the governor is a ceremonial position, but in the case of NWFP, the governor is charged with directly administering FATA on behalf of the president.

Table 2. Provincial Government Leaders

NAME	OFFICE	POLITICAL PARTY	PHONE NUMBER
Amir Haider Khan Hoti	Chief Minister	ANP	0937 865656
Owais Ahmed Ghani	Governor	ANP	N/A
Kiramat Ullah Khan	Speaker	PPP	0300 9508525 0333 9399850
Khushdil Khan	Deputy Speaker	ANP	091 2370909 0300 5887691
Syed Ahmad Hussain Shah	Minster: Industry	PPP	091 9212942
Amjid Khan Afridi	Minister: Housing	ANP	0345 8300005 0300 8150005
Barrister Arshad Abdullah	Minister: Law	ANP	0300 8597808 091 6511985
Bashir Ahmad Bilour	Senior Minister: Local Government and Rural Development	ANP	0915275388 091 5276388
Al Hajj Habib ur Rehman Tanoli	Minister: Revenue	Independent	0997 302998 0300 5539163
Haji Hidayat Ullah Khan	Minister: Livestock	ANP	091 9210370 0300 9034448
Mian Iftikhar Hussain	Minister: Information and Public Relations	ANP	091 9213490 0333 9103555
Liaqat Ali Shabab	Minister: Excise and Taxation	PPP	091 9212917 0300 5903394
Mahmood Zaib Khan	Minister: Technical Education	PPP	0300 5749256 0346 9399099
Qazi Muhammad Asad Khan	Minister: Higher Education	ANP	0995 612354 0300 8553263
Muhammad Ayub Khan	Minister: Science and Information Technology	ANP	0345 9841111

NAME	OFFICE	POLITICAL PARTY	PHONE NUMBER
Arbab Muhammad Ayyub Jan	Minister: Agriculture	ANP	091 9210348
Muhammad Hamayun Khan	Minister: Finance	PPP	0345 9403443 0300 5700888
Muhammad Shuja Khan	Minister: Food	PPP	091 9210043 0300 811001
Muhammad Zarshid	Minister: Zakat and Usher	ANP	091 9210366
Namroz Khan	Minister: Hajj & Auqaf	ANP	091 9213493
Mian Nisar Gul Kaka Khel	Minister: Prisons	ANP	091 5273370
Pervaiz Khattak	Minister: Irrigation	PPP	0300 8583450
Rahim Dad Khan	Senior Minister: Planning & Development	PPP	0300 939363
Saleem Khan	Minister: Population Welfare	PPP	0302 8060430
Sardar Hussain	Minister: School & Literacy	ANP	0304 9890325
Sitara Ayaz	Minister: Social Welfare	ANP	0300 5869988
Haji Sher Azam Khan Wazir	Minister: Labor	PPP	0300 5005359
Syed Zahir Ali Shah	Minister: Health	PPP	091 221888182
Wajid Ali Khan	Minister: Forest	ANP	0300 5742002
Syed Syed Aqil Shah	Minister: Sports, Culture, and Tourism	ANP	0345 9091918

Table 3. List of NWFP Secretaries

NAME OF OFFICER	PRESENT POSTING	PHONE NO
Mr. Javed Iqbal	Chief Secretary	091 9210666
Mr. Ghulam Dastgir	ACS P&D	091 9210344
Mr. Mian Sahib Jan	Secretary, Establishment	091 9210349
Mr. Fayyaz Khan Toru	Secretary, Home & Tribal Affairs	091 9211121
Mr. Ahsanullah Khan	SMBR	091 9210328
Mr. Faheem Ullah Khattak	Secretary, Finance	091 9210443
Mr. Sajid Khan Jadoon	Secretary, E&T	091 9212659
Mr. Zafar Iqbal	Secretary, Transport	091 9212557
Arbab Muhammad Arif	Secretary to Governor	091 9211716
Mr. Fazal Rehmani	Secretary, Housing	091 9212430
Mr. Tarik Jamil	Principal Sec. to Chief Minister	091 9211705
Mr. M. Riaz Khan	Secretary, Water and Sanitation	091 9210859
Mr. M.Asfaq Khan	Secretary, Irrigation	091 9210845
Mr. Attaullah Khan	Secretary, Agri. & Livestock	091 9210025
Mr. Azmat Hanif Orakzai	Secretary, Information	091 9210365
Mr. Sahibzada Fazal Amin	Secretary, Sports, Culture & Tourism Dept.	091 9212086
Mr. Nauman Shah Jadoon	Secretary, Haj and Auqaf	091 9210203
Qazi Hifzer Rehman	Secretary, Food	091 9213255
Mr. Owais Agha	Secretary, Environment	091 9210333
Mr. Shah Sahib	Secretary, Social Welfare, Zakat	091 9211391
Dr. Syed Sohail Altaf	Secretary, Health	091 9210342

NAME OF OFFICER	PRESENT POSTING	PHONE NO
Mr. Shah Wali Khan	Secretary, Industries	091 9210924
Mr. Farooq Sarwar	Secretary, Law	091 9210023
Col. (R) Ghulam Hussain	Secretary, Admin	091 9210947
Mr. Muhammad Ikram	Secretary, P&D	091 9210410
Mr. Hifzur Rehman	Secretary, LG&RD	091 9210026
Mr. Muhammad Arifeen	Secretary, E&S Education	091 9210480
Mr. Ahmad Hanif Orakzai	Secretary, Higher Education	091 9210337
Mr. Amjad Shahid Afridi	Secretary, ST & IT	091 9212400
Maj. (R) Muzaffar Ali Afridi	Secretary, Population Welfare	091 9211535
Mr. Humayun Khan	Inter-Provincial Coordination Department	091 9212325
Mr. Zahur Ahmad Khalil	Energy & Power Department	091 9213820

The Provincial Assembly of NWFP, the only province-wide elected body, has 124 elected members. There are 99 regular seats, 22 seats reserved for women, and three seats reserved for non-Muslims. The official website of the assembly (*www.panwfp.gov.pk*) contains contact details of all the members along with details of ongoing and previous legislative work.

A chief secretary heads the bureaucratic set-up of the province, coordinating and supervising functions of various departments, which are themselves headed by secretaries.

The *zila nazim* (elected mayor) heads the district government and is assisted by the district coordination officer (DCO). While acting as the manager-in-chief of the district, the zila nazim requires zila council support for major budgetary approvals. Various officers dealing with district revenue collection, education, healthcare, police, and law enforcement function under the supervision of, or in close coordination with, the district government. Though some districts (Malakand, Swat, and Buner for instance) are called Provincially Administered Tribal Areas (PATA), they stand largely amalgamated within the provincial system and they enjoy no special status in terms of administrative functioning.

Before 2001, various districts were grouped together to form a division headed by a commissioner (from the civil service), but the system was dissolved with the advent of elected mayors of districts. However, the old division system is again being resurrected to improve the administrative capacity of the provincial government.

Table 4. Political Parties in the Provincial Assembly

POLITICAL PARTIES	ELECTED	RESERVED	TOTAL
Awami National Party (ANP)	30	8	38
Pakistan People's Party (Shaheed Bhutto)	16	4	20
Muttahida Majilis-e Amal (JUI-F)	11	3	14
Pakistan Muslim League (Nawaz)	6	1	7
Pakistan Muslim League (Quaid)	5	1	6
Pakistan People's Party (Sherpao)	5	1	6
Independents	26	7	33
Total Seats	**99**	**25**	**124**

Major Political Parties

Awami National Party (ANP): The party of the legendary Pashtun leader Abdul Ghaffar Khan, the ANP was formed in 1986 as a successor to the National Awami Party (NAP). The NAP was the first major opposition party created after Pakistan's independence that sought to rally nationalist and democratic forces. Today, the ANP is associated with Pashtun nationalism and secular politics. It is currently active in NWFP, as well as Pashtun-dominated areas of Baluchistan and the city of Karachi. However, NWFP politics remains its primary focus. In the 2008 elections, it emerged as the major political force, sizably defeating religious political forces. Nevertheless, just short of numbers to form a government on its own, the ANP formed a coalition government with the PPP. In turn, the ANP is part of the coalition in the federal government where its representatives have three cabinet positions. The ANP has six seats in the 100-member Pakistani Senate, providing it with additional political leverage in national policies directed towards NWFP.

Pakistan People's Party (PPP): The left-leaning PPP was set up in 1967 by a group of intellectuals and politicians led by Zulfikar Ali Bhutto in reaction to the military dictatorship of General Ayub Khan. The PPP has since emerged as one of the strongest political parties of Pakistan, with a support base in every province. It formed governments from 1971-77, 1988-90, and 1993-96. Currently, the PPP is the leading partner in the national coalition government under Prime Minister Yousaf Raza Gilani, and the PPP's co-chairperson, Asif Ali Zardari (widower of Benazir Bhutto), is the president of the country.

Pakistan Muslim League (Nawaz) – PML-N: The Muslim League was a conservative political party that spearheaded the movement for an independent Pakistan in the 1940s. Since Pakistan's creation, it has taken many shapes and has split into many factions. Former Prime Minister Nawaz Sharif created the Nawaz faction in 1993. While most of its support is in Punjab province, it has support in NWFP, especially among the Hindko speakers of Abbottabad, Haripur, and Mansehra districts. It remained part of provincial coalition governments in the 1990s.

Pakistan Muslim League (Quaid-e Azam) – PML-Q: In the lead-up to the 2002 national elections under President Pervez Musharraf's rule, many members of the Muslim League (Nawaz) split to form this new faction, allegedly at the behest of the intelligence services who were tasked to create a "king's party." Punjabi leader Chaudhry Shujaat Husain led this faction, but it has limited political support in NWFP.

Muttihada Majlis-e Amal (MMA or United Action Forum): Configured as a loose coalition of six Islamist parties formed for the 2002 elections, the MMA no longer functions as originally conceived. Given the changing political realities of NWFP, however, it could reemerge in the future. Its largest constituent is the Jamaat-e Islami (JI), founded by Maulana Maududi in 1941 and considered to be Pakistan's best organized religious party. Another of its long-standing Islamist parties, the Jamiat Ulema-e Islam (JUI – Party of the Religious Scholars/ Clerics), is associated with madrassas that gave rise to the Afghan Taliban movement in the early 1990s. JUI has two factions – one led by Maulana Fazlur Rahman of Dera Ismail Khan (JUI –F), and the other by Maulana Sami ul Haq of Nowshera district (JUI – S). Both factions are conservative advocates of a central role for Islam and sharia in national governance, and both have controversial reputations due to their corrupt practices when a part of the NWFP government from 2002-07. Both also strongly oppose Westernization in its socioeconomic and cultural forms. While these parties enjoy considerable street power and were strengthened by General Zia ul Haq's policies of the 1980s, their electoral turnout has mostly been dismal. Interestingly, Sufi/ Barelvi-oriented Jamiat Ulema-e Pakistan (JUP) and the Shia Tehrik-e Jafaria (TEJ) were also part of MMA, though they were not given much representation in the government after the MMA victory in 2002.

RADICALIZATION

The rise of the TTP (Tehrik-eTaliban Pakistan – Movement for Taliban in Pakistan) and similar extremist groups in FATA and NWFP has cut into the support base of mainstream religious parties, especially the JI and the JUI-F, as well as its faction led by Sami ul Haq. While both groups share some common political agendas regarding sharia and the West, they are pursuing different goals: the TTP and the TNSM (Tehrik-e Nifaz-e Shariati Mohammadi – Movement for Enforcement of Sharia) want to enforce their views at all costs, whereas the JI and the JUI-F believe and take part in electoral politics. The religious youth are increasingly finding militant groups more attractive because they see a ray of hope in defiance against the system. Fewer education and job opportunities and worsening economic trends may have engendered hopelessness among the young.

PAKISTANI LEADERSHIP AND NWFP

The important Pakistani players see the current crisis through many different lenses. The new civilian government under President Zardari favors increasing cooperation with Afghanistan, development efforts along the border, and strong action against the militants. The civilian approach is constrained by the Pakistani military and its focus on countering India. This extends to suspicions about Indian influence in Afghanistan and Pakistan and the usefulness of militants in Kashmir and elsewhere. In the wake of India-Pakistan tensions over the Mumbai terror attacks, Taliban and militant fighters declared they would join hands with the Pakistani army to defend the country against India. At the same time, the senior army leadership has no sympathy for militants who target the army or for militant overreach beyond their traditional centers of power, as shown by army operations against TTP and extremists in the Bajaur and Swat areas. The army still has little interest in challenging extremism at its root in Waziristan.

NWFP's economy is largely based on agriculture. However, the mountainous terrain of the province is not suited to extensive cultivation. Canals, tube wells, and lift irrigation schemes irrigate the land with water from the Indus, Kabul, and Swat Rivers.

PHOTO BY BILL SPENSE

Chapter 5
The Economy

T he insecurity and violence of the past 30 years has transformed NWFP's economy from one based on tourism and agriculture to one that is dominated by an informal economy of smuggling imports, drugs, and humans. While the size of NWFP's economy is small, the parallel informal economy is believed by regional experts to be around four or five times the size of the formal economy. According to Pakistani economists, some of the underlying factors for NWFP's economic underperformance and problems are geographic in nature, while others are structural constraints.

MAJOR ECONOMIC HUBS

Peshawar: As the capital of NWFP and the province's largest city, Peshawar is a natural economic hub. Currently, the service, trading, retail, and industrial sectors have a large presence in the city. Peshawar's large-scale industry is in the engineering, wood, and marble sectors.

Bannu: The district's central market serves the entire "southern region" of NWFP. Bannu also potentially provides the shortest trade route to the Central Asian markets.

Haripur: Located in mainstream Pakistan, this is one of the most developed districts of NWFP. In the rural areas, agriculture is the main driver of the economy, whereas there is a large industrial base (both private and public) in and around a number of urban centers.

Kohat: The district is notorious for being the second-busiest smuggling route between Pakistan and Afghanistan (the other is the Khyber agency).

Mardan: Most tobacco factories are based in the Mardan area. Besides local brands, the Mardan and Swabi tobacco factories are well known for producing fake cigarettes of foreign brands.

Swat: Before 2009, Swat was a tourism hub. However, the wave of militancy and the military's response have almost destroyed the tourism sector.

INFORMAL ECONOMY

A major contraband trade has grown around products imported into Afghanistan (through the Karachi seaport) and smuggled back into the markets of NWFP, especially in Peshawar and the surrounding districts. These are mostly transported back into Pakistan through FATA's Khyber agency and adjoining areas through pickup vans (where mud tracks are available) and otherwise on the backs of donkeys and camels through difficult mountainous routes. No customs duty is paid on imports this way because of the UN-facilitated Afghan Transit Trade Agreement (ATTA). Peshawar's famous Kharkhano Market (a shopping plaza), with around 4,500 shops, is the major hub of this activity. The Bara market (in Khyber Agency) was the center of such activity but the market was closed due to military operation in the Bara area in 2007-08.

The principal imported products in this category are electronic equipment, air conditioners, garments, cosmetics, automobile spare parts, mobile phones, and even vehicle tires. Because of highly competitive prices, people from outside NWFP also visit Peshawar and Nowshera for shopping.

During the Taliban era (1995-2001), Pakistan cracked down on this illegal trade pattern by imposing a ban on a list of 24 items that Afghanistan was not allowed to import under the ATTA, including television sets and cosmetics. The situation changed after the fall of Taliban regime in late 2001. Afghanistan again imports these items, largely benefitting NWFP traders. No taxes are paid on these by the trader community as there are no records of these products being imported.

FORMAL ECONOMY

NWFP's GDP is estimated to be 18 billion rupees (US $250 million). Most of the general population engages in subsistence farming. Wheat, corn (maize), sugar cane, and tobacco are the major crops of the agricultural industry. Yet the province does not produce enough output for local requirements. For example, NWFP imports 90 percent of its wheat, the staple food of over 21 million people of the province who consume around 3.5 million metric tons annually.

The principal manufacturing sectors are sugar processing, vegetable ghee, cement, cigarettes, safety matches, and paper. Other products are cotton textiles, fertilizer, petroleum, and chemicals. However, the recent wave of militancy and insurgency in NWFP has badly affected the industrial sector in the province. In 2008-09 alone, about 843 factories closed down. According to a January 2009 public statement by the Sarhad Chamber of Commerce based in Peshawar, "there are about 2,500 factories in the province and only 594 of these are functional." Most recently, by April 2009, 287 out of 317 small factories had closed down in the Swat district alone in response to the lawlessness and violence.

Table 5. Agriculture

MAJOR CROPS	AREA (THOUSAND HECTARES)	PRODUCTION (THOUSAND TONNES)	YIELD PER HECTARE (KG)
wheat	609	957	1,571
Maize	444	709	1,597
Rice	48	100	2,083
Sugarcane	97	4,396	45,320
Gram	38	20	526
Tobacco	36	91	2,528
Barley	17	18	1,059

Source: NWFP Bureau of Statistics, http://nwfp.gov.pk/BOS/nwfpfigure05.htm.

Table 6. Manufacturing (2005-06)

TYPE OF INDUSTRIES	NO. OF REPORTING UNITS (2005-06)	EMPLOYMENT LEVEL NOS. (2005-06)	PRODUCTION	
			2004-05	2005-06
Sugar (Thousand Tonnes)	3	1,271	104	94
Vegetable Ghee (Thousand Tonnes)	14	1,201	279	353
Cement (Thousand Tonnes)	4	1,083	4,632	5,136
Cigarettes (Million)	5	871	15,918	17,364
Safety Matches (Million Boxes)	11	1,710	2,630	4,036
Paper (Thousand Tonnes)	2	208	8	7

Source: NWFP Bureau of Statistics, http://nwfp.gov.pk/BOS/nwfpfigure05.htm.

NWFP's tourism industry sprang from the natural beauty of the region. Swat district, sometimes referred to as Asia's Switzerland, was once a popular center of Pakistan's tourism industry. Tourism also drives the economy of Mansehra district. According to the NWFP Tourism Department, the overall tourism in NWFP has declined by about 50 percent since 2006-07. The worst hit areas are Swat and Malakand, though Mansehra has also been affected, especially by the 2005 earthquake. Still, Chitral tourism has not been influenced by the security deterioration in NWFP. Travels of international tourists to NWFP, especially from the West, have almost come to a complete halt due to the increasing Taliban threat in NWFP.

ECONOMIC CONSTRAINTS

Terrain

Although an agriculture-based economy, NWFP's mountainous terrain is not suited to sustain extensive agricultural cultivation. Of the 25.4 million total acres in NWFP, only 6.55 million acres are arable. Irrigation is carried out on about one-third of the cultivated land. At present, an area of 2.27 million acres is irrigated through canals, tube wells, lift irrigation schemes, and civil canal systems.

Transport

Currently, transportation of goods and services is difficult because of limited road access and the poor condition of the road network, especially in rural areas. The difficulty of transport prevents or reduces access to markets, education and health facilities, and other social opportunities for a large percentage of the population.

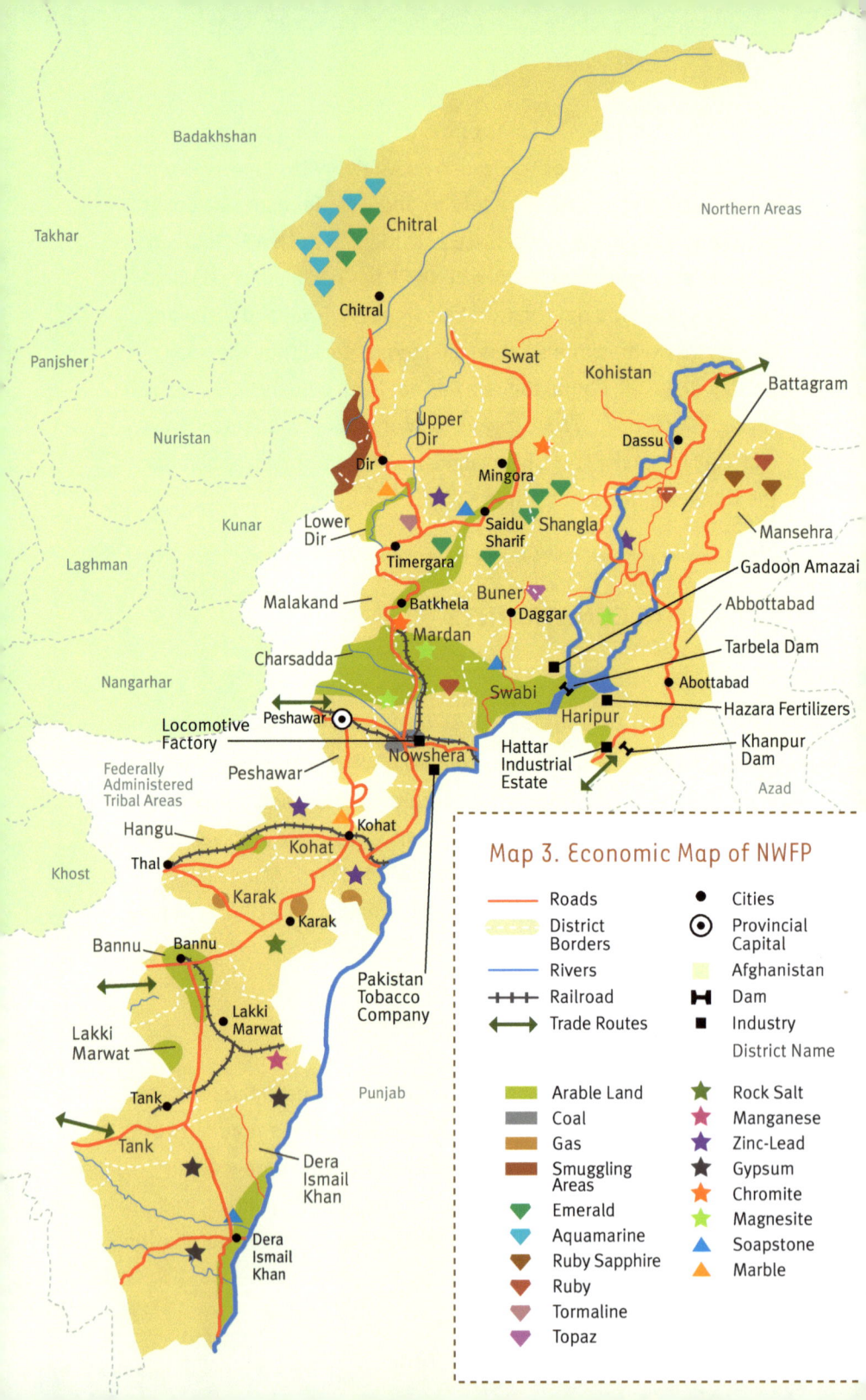

Map 3. Economic Map of NWFP

Legend:

- Roads
- District Borders
- Rivers
- Railroad
- Trade Routes
- Cities
- Provincial Capital
- Afghanistan
- Dam
- Industry
- District Name

- Arable Land
- Coal
- Gas
- Smuggling Areas
- Emerald
- Aquamarine
- Ruby Sapphire
- Ruby
- Tormaline
- Topaz

- Rock Salt
- Manganese
- Zinc-Lead
- Gypsum
- Chromite
- Magnesite
- Soapstone
- Marble

Place labels:

Badakhshan, Takhar, Panjsher, Nuristan, Kunar, Laghman, Nangarhar, Khost, Northern Areas

Chitral, Chitral, Swat, Kohistan, Battagram, Upper Dir, Dir, Mingora, Dassu, Mansehra, Lower Dir, Saidu Sharif, Shangla, Gadoon Amazai, Timergara, Buner, Abbottabad, Malakand, Batkhela, Daggar, Tarbela Dam, Charsadda, Mardan, Abbottabad, Swabi, Hazara Fertilizers, Locomotive Factory, Peshawar, Haripur, Khanpur Dam, Peshawar, Nowshera, Hattar Industrial Estate, Azad

Federally Administered Tribal Areas, Hangu, Kohat, Kohat, Thal, Karak, Karak, Bannu, Bannu, Lakki Marwat, Lakki Marwat, Tank, Tank, Dera Ismail Khan, Dera Ismail Khan, Pakistan Tobacco Company, Punjab

Additionally, the deep inland location of NWFP translates into high transport costs into and out of the province for regional trade.

Violence and Insecurity

For the past three decades, NWFP has been at the frontline of battles, starting with the Soviet invastion of Afghanistan in 1979. The volatile situation on the borders and in FATA has been accompanied by insecurity that discourages private investment. The constant inflow of refugees from FATA and Afghanistan has drained the province's weak social and economic infrastructure. The Swat crisis and the consequent massive movement of internally displaced persons (IDPs) have created further strain.

Human Capital

Pakistani economists believe that poverty in NWFP is closely associated with a lack of human capital, measured by education and literacy levels. NWFP net primary enrollment rates of 40 percent for girls and 53 percent for boys are both below the Pakistani averages of 48 percent (girls) and 56 percent (boys). The below-average education is reflected in the workforce, which is largely illiterate (65 percent) and unskilled.

Trade Barriers

Between 2001 and 2006, Pakistan's exports to Afghanistan grew from $221 million to $1.2 billion. Despite this growth, NWFP has not been able to capitalize on the market due to various legal and constitutional hurdles. The government of NWFP has not let its products be directly exported to Afghanistan.

Most rural roads in NWFP are in poor condition, reducing people's access to markets, schools, health facilities, and other social opportunities. Road projects aim to improve transit for both military and civilian traffic.

PHOTO BY ANTHONY MAW

Chapter 6
Infrastructure and
International Assistance

N WFP's economic status is directly linked to its underdeveloped infrastructure. Poor quality and inaccessible infrastructure isolate the province and severely inhibits economic development. Ad hoc international aid projects are implemented across NWFP, especially regarding repairing and improving road infrastructure destroyed in the 2005 earthquake. However, these infrastructure improvements are co-opted by both the Taliban and the Pakistani military, who continue to constrict trade and economic development.

INFRASTRUCTURE

Transportation

NWFP has a road network of about 15,400 km, which represents roughly 16 percent of the total road network of about 260,000 km in Pakistan. Most roads in rural NWFP are in a poor condition, but major road networks connecting major cities of NWFP are in comparatively better condition. Because 83 percent of the population is rural, the limited road access and poor condition of the road network prevent or reduce access to markets, education and health facilities, and other social opportunities to a large percentage of the population.

The Kohat Pass is very dangerous for long vehicles (e.g., trailers) because of sharp turns. To facilitate trade, the Kohat Tunnel was recently completed to provide an alternate route connecting Peshawar to the southern tribal agencies. Because the Kohat Tunnel connects the capital to the southern agencies, it is now seen as a strategic link by both Taliban militants and the Pakistan military and changes control frequently, limiting the economic utility.

Water Sector

There is a serious water crisis in NWFP, though the situation is better in comparison to the adjacent Punjab province. Due to the agrarian economy of the province, water scarcity seriously affects crop productivity, especially in the districts of Dera Ismail Khan, Tank, Bannu, Karak, and Kohat. The situation is better in Charsada, Nowshera, and Haripur, where water resources from major dams in the area benefit the agricultural sector. The overall water crisis has not been tackled by successive NWFP governments. With UNICEF support, a Water Supply and Sanitation (WATSAN) cell was set up in NWFP's Local Government and Rural Development Department in March 2009. Distribution of water from the Indus River between Punjab province and NWFP is also a perennial issue, and various efforts have failed to bridge the differences. The Kalabagh Dam issue, discussed later in this chapter, is also relevant to the water issue.

Energy and Electricity

Pakistan is facing an acute shortage of electricity and long hours of load shedding are routine in NWFP. The current power demand of 1,997 megawatts (MW) in NWFP is expected to rise to around 7,000

MW in 15 years, and about 1,550-1,700 MW is currently available in different seasons. The fact that the NWFP government is working on the feasibility of 20 small dams in the province indicates the nature of energy shortage in the province. The Ghazi Barotha Hydropower Project (near Tarbela Dam in the Haripur area) eased pressure on NWFP energy demands in recent years, but a gap clearly still exists. The NWFP government also provides subsidies for installation of alternative energy plants as a solution, and 184 biogas plants were installed in Nowshera, Charsada, and Abbottabad districts in the 2007-09 timeframe.

NWFP has a huge potential for small hydropower plants that can be operated at the community level in the areas where running water is available in sufficient quantity. Such plants have already been installed in major parts of northern areas that are adjacent to Chitral district. Pakistan Council of Renewable Energy Technologies (PCRET) claims that it set up 409 micro-hydro plants in NWFP in recent years. The installation cost of a one-kilowatt plant is between Rs 80,000-90,000 (US $1,000-1,100) and is enough to provide electricity to at least five medium-sized houses.

RECENT EVENTS

NWFP's infrastructure was badly damaged by the 2005 earthquake. About 6,600 km of roads in Abbottabad, Battagram, Kohistan, Mansehra, and Shangla were severely damaged.

Kalabagh Dam is a multi-purpose hydroelectricity and irrigation project that could add 2,400 MW of generation capacity for Pakistan. Although in Punjab, not in NWFP, the dam reservoir will inundate the upstream province of NWFP and could flood over existing infrastructure. The people of NWFP see the dam as a risk to irrigate the desert lands in

Punjab, mostly owned by top civil-military personnel. NWFP resistance has stalled the project and it remains a divisive issue between NWFP and Islamabad.

INTERNATIONAL AID

Several international aid projects are targeted at improving the physical and social infrastructure. These projects are all in varying stages of implementation:

Trade: The US Trade and Development Agency, together with the Planning Commission of Pakistan and the Ministry of Finance of Afghanistan, signed a memorandum of understanding in May 2009 agreeing to pursue a Pakistan-Afghanistan Infrastructure and Trade Initiative. The plan seeks to foster economic development in the region and promote trade with Afghanistan.

Electricity: The UNDP's Global Environment Facility (GEF) signed a contract with the Pakistani government in May 2009 for the implementation of $19.2 million plan to set up mini-hydro power plants in Chitral.

Education: Six international donor agencies agreed to finance the education sector plan that the provincial government devised for improving indicators in the education sector and achieving the United Nations Millennium Development Goals. A memorandum of understanding for that purpose was signed in April 2009 by officials of the NWFP government and representatives of partner agencies, raising hopes for future foreign assistance that was on decline for a couple of years in the province.

Health and Emergency Services: In 2007, the US Agency for International Development (USAID) donated four ambulances to the districts of Upper Dir and Buner in NWFP. The ambulances, donated under the USAID-funded Pakistan Initiative for Mothers and Newborns (PAIMAN) project, are specially designed and equipped to assist pregnant women and newborns.

Transportation and Roads: The World Bank financed the reconstruction of the roads damaged by the 2005 earthquake through its Highway Rehabilitation Project.

The security forces of NWFP are under-resourced. While the average Pakistani earns about $125 a month, members of the NWFP security forces are paid only $50 per month. By comparison, Taliban militants are paid around $150 per month.

PHOTO BY ANTHONY MAW

Chapter 7
Security Issues

Extremism and violence are on the rise in NWFP due to the growing influence of the Taliban and the unchallenged militant domination of FATA. Years of neglect and poor governance helped create conditions for extremism to prosper. Due to increasing violence against Pakistani security forces and government targets and militant expansion in NWFP's Swat Valley and other districts in 2008, Islamabad's long-standing disinterest in taking on Islamic militants became untenable. In 2009, the Pakistani Army finally took strong action against the militants in NWFP, but the Taliban continued to contest control of many areas of NWFP (and retain control in FATA).

Militants have launched some 700 terrorist attacks in NWFP between January 2008 and June 2009, including several dozen suicide attacks. While attacks in FATA target the government, NWFP attacks have a more ideological focus. For instance, targets included a welfare office in Swabi, hundreds of girls' schools, Swat's Buthgarh Jehanabad historical site (containing rocks engraved with Buddhist images), women's rights activists, video and music shops, and, at times, barber shops (due to their practice of shaving beards, which extremists consider un-Islamic). Militants have warned women not to appear in public without a veil and to avoid visiting the marketplace.

Of NWFP's 24 districts, the national government declared eight districts as high security zones in the latter half of 2008: Peshawar, Mardan, Kohat, Bannu, Dera Ismail Khan, Nowshera, Abbottabad, and Tank. Five of these districts (or their frontier regions) border different FATA agencies. There does not appear to be an immediate threat of Taliban takeover in Peshawar, despite some media reports, but extremist militias in NWFP are increasingly targeting Peshawar for attacks and intimidation.

Attacks against Shia Muslims have also increased in NWFP, especially in Dera Ismail Khan and Peshawar districts. This trend is closely linked with the sectarian conflict in FATA's Kurram agency and to a lesser degree Orakzai agency. Since traditional militant Wahhabis view the Shia as religious apostates, Shia are widely considered anti-Taliban in FATA and NWFP. Though the Shia have their own extremists and militants, they are believed to have taken part in some of the anti-Taliban operations in FATA. There is also evidence that Iran financially supports some Shia groups in FATA and NWFP.

PAKISTANI SECURITY FORCES IN NWFP

Pakistan's 550,000-man army is oriented toward a conventional war with India – not a counterinsurgency fight in the tribal areas. Until recently, the army largely stayed clear of the Taliban, leaving border area security to the Frontier Corps. The British colonial rulers developed the Frontier Corps (FC) as a tribal paramilitary force that acts to provide border security and law enforcement. The FC is led and commanded by officers from the regular Pakistani army, but the oversight of this organization rests with the Ministry of the Interior. Their tribal links and connections bind them strongly to the inhabitants of NWFP, and they bring familiarity with the local dialects, people, and tribes. However, they sometimes desert when ordered to take action against members of their own tribe. An estimated 120,000 Pakistani army and 50,000 Frontier Corps troops are deployed in NWFP and FATA.

Funding for security forces in NWFP is a problem. The average Pakistani earns some Rs. 10,000 (US $125) a month. Army soldiers in Pakistan earn about Rs. 8000 (US $100) and receive benefits including health-care and lodging. According to credible media reports, Taliban militants are paid Rs. 12,000 by their leadership. However, FC troops are paid a meager monthly salary of around Rs. 4,000 (US $50). Pakistan has also received funds from the US for the reform and upgrade of the FC since 2007-08. A total of $750 million will be disbursed to train and modernize the FC.

NWFP's 55,000-member police force mans 217 police stations. This translates to one police station for every 133 square miles of some of the world's most dangerous terrain. They are under-resourced in both manpower and equipment. The police have little credibility, and residents do not believe the police are capable or willing to challenge the Taliban's expanding influence. This belief was reinforced when large numbers of Swat police deserted after Maulana Fazlullah (the leader of militants in the Swat area) told the local police to give up their jobs or face the Taliban's wrath. In January 2009, the US Embassy in Islamabad announced its plan to provide $4.1 million worth of police equipment to NWFP, including troop carriers, motorcycles, ballistic helmets, and bulletproof vests.

Pakistan's Inter-Services Intelligence (ISI) agency has an entangled and controversial role with tribal militants. The ISI channeled funds (from the CIA and Saudi Arabia) to the Taliban and other militant groups in the tribal areas during the Soviet-Afghan war. After 9/11, Musharraf changed government policy and stopped supporting the Taliban. However, the ISI had forged close ties with the Taliban during their 30-year alliance.

There are disputed reports that elements of the ISI or former ISI continue to support the Taliban. Evidence suggests that ISI support ranges from retired ISI operatives assisting the Taliban to Pakistan's ability to easily round up high-level Taliban targets in a short amount of time (such as in

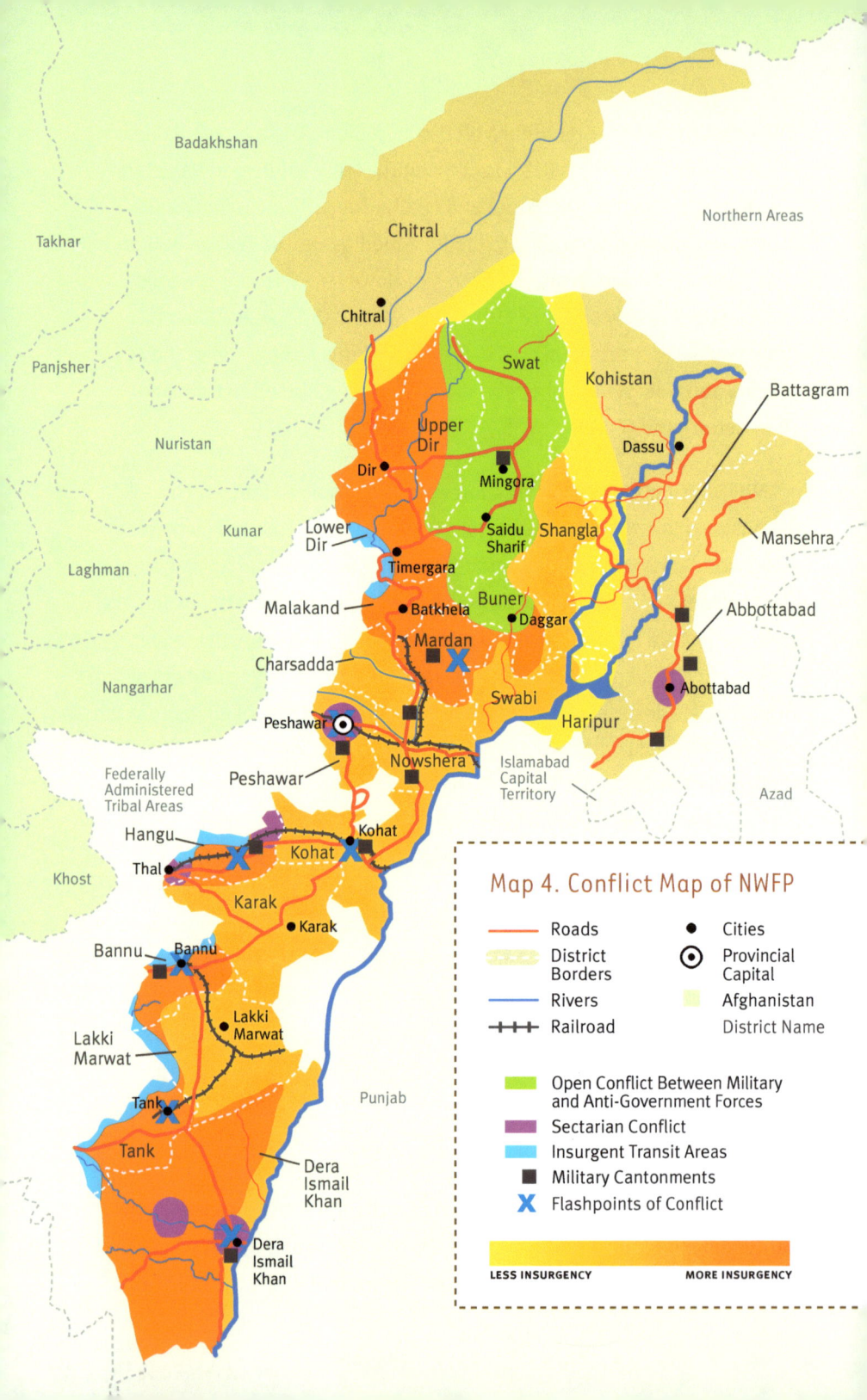

Map 4. Conflict Map of NWFP

Legend:
- Roads
- District Borders
- Rivers
- Railroad
- Cities
- Provincial Capital
- Afghanistan
- District Name

- Open Conflict Between Military and Anti-Government Forces
- Sectarian Conflict
- Insurgent Transit Areas
- Military Cantonments
- Flashpoints of Conflict

LESS INSURGENCY — MORE INSURGENCY

Quetta in February 2007). The ease with which the arrests have happened have suggested that while no covert support of the Taliban may exist, the ISI and Pakistani army have not made a concerted effort to eradicate them either. ISI members may be divided on the issue.

THE TALIBAN

The relatively new and growing militant power in Pakistan is Tehrik-e Taliban Pakistan (TTP, or Movement for Taliban in Pakistan), perhaps best understood as a loose coalition of religiously-inspired militant groups. TTP is strongest in FATA but has made inroads in various parts of NWFP in 2008. The TTP expansion was more tangible in the districts of Bannu, Dera Ismail Khan, Karak, Kohat, Tank, Lower and Upper Dir, and Buner. Peshawar, the capital city of NWFP, also came under a significant threat from militant groups operating in the adjacent Khyber agency of FATA.

There are an estimated 100,000 Taliban insurgents in NWFP and FATA. Many NWFP residents are sympathetic to extremist groups or are conservative and anti-Western in outlook. In considering total armed men, consider that almost every Pashtun has a weapon and that there is considerable animosity towards Pakistani forces and US/NATO forces across the border. While NWFP is less isolated and more moderate than FATA overall, there are hard-line extremists in both areas.

A *shura* (consultative body) of 40 senior Taliban leaders set up the TTP as an umbrella organization in December 2007. Militant commander Baitullah Mehsud was appointed as its *amir* (leader), Maulana Hafiz Gul Bahadur of North Waziristan as senior *naib amir* (deputy), and Maulana Faqir Muhammad of Bajaur agency as the third in command. The shura not only has representation from all of FATA's seven tribal agencies, but also from the settled NWFP districts of Swat, Bannu, Tank, Lakki Marwat, Dera Ismail Khan, Kohistan, Buner, and Malakand. Rahman Malik, Pakistan's Interior

Minister, publicly acknowledged that the TTP is "an extension of al-Qaeda" and that the two organizations have close ties.

Since its establishment, the TTP has announced the following objectives and principles:

- enforcing sharia;
- uniting against NATO forces in Afghanistan and performing "defensive jihad" against the Pakistani army;
- reacting strongly if military operations are not stopped in Swat district and North Waziristan agency;
- demanding the abolition of all military checkpoints in the FATA area and the release of *Lal Masjid* (Red Mosque) Imam Abdul Aziz; and
- refusing future peace deals with the national government.

The Taliban have also sought to assume the role of police in certain districts (such as Tank), with Taliban patrols and even trials. This has a corrosive effect on the legitimacy of the Pakistani government.

2008-2009 EXTREMIST AND TALIBAN EMERGENCE IN SWAT DISTRICT

The 2008 emergence of extremist Islamic opposition in the Swat Valley has had a critical impact in turning the Pakistani government's attention toward the risks of extremism in the border areas. During 2008, the Islamic militant group TNSM in Swat under Sufi Mohammad and his son Fazlullah grew in strength and drew closer links with Taliban militants in FATA. Murder and kidnapping became a daily routine in 2008 and the Pakistani government did little, while local law enforcement and civil administration were overwhelmed. The May 2009 report by the Human Rights Commission of Pakistan indicated instances where evidently the army and the ISI not only remained aloof from the people, but also used their influence to save Fazlullah and his collaborators from local police. Military action was started in the area later in 2008 but the situation remained tense.

Late in 2008, a "peace deal" was arranged with the understanding that Mohammad would disarm his cadres and bring Fazlullah into the mainstream. The project failed in the first few months of 2009 after Mohammad made extremist statements challenging the democratic government and vowed to expand sharia law from Swat throughout Pakistan. Fazlullah's group refused to give up arms. The government responded with a major military operation in the beginning of May 2009. Hundreds of TNSM and TTP militants were killed and arrested, and a major humanitarian crisis erupted due to the fighting. By June 2009, about three million people from Swat, Buner, and Dir had been displaced.

The Pakistani army conducted simultaneous operations in Dir in the southwest and Buner to the east, while the Special Services Group (SGG) Commandos blocked the Taliban's fallback area towards the north in Peochar Valley. Mingora City and Saidu Sharif saw major urban battles. As of June 2009, the army was winning the conflict. Public and political support strengthened the military leadership's ability to take decisive action. The army's integrity and counterinsurgency skills will be tested by the speed with which they can defeat Taliban in Swat.

The Taliban takeover and government counteroffensive in Swat district displaced millions to other parts of NWFP and Pakistan. Many militants from the Swat area moved to adjacent districts of Mardan and Swabi after the government counteroffensive in May 2008. The primary target of the government was the TTP umbrella group TNSM. A few dozen foreign fighters (mostly Arab and Uzbek) also moved to the Swat area and are working closely with Fazlullah cadres. Fazlullah himself had joined the TTP umbrella group, though the TNSM faction working directly under Sufi Mohammad has largely remained independent of the TTP.

VOANews.com

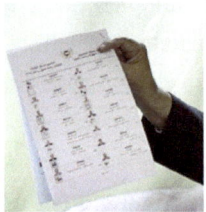

Television, internet, radio, and print media all serve English, Urdu, and Pashto speakers of NWFP. Voice of America airs a six-hour program of news and information in all three languages. However, extremists have primarily used radio as a means to broadcast their message, transmitting on illegal frequencies. www.voanews.com/pashto

Chapter 8
Information and Media Influence

Although electronic and print media are accessible in the NWFP, radio transmissions remain a widespread source of news and information, and both legal and illegal channels operate in the region. Illegal stations are of significant concern because they are used by the TTP and their allies to reach the local population, spread fundamentalism, and promote violence. Although many of these illegal stations were shut down in 2006, Pakistani efforts to counter the spread of unlicensed FM transmitters are largely ineffectual, and the TTP continue to broadcast to the local population.

Mainstream private and public media are available in NWFP and include television, internet, print, and radio communications in English, Urdu, and Pashto. Currently, there are around 50 independent news and entertainment channels broadcasting electronic media in Pakistan. Around 30 of these channels broadcast regular news and current affairs programs. State-controlled media provide the main source of information for the 70 percent of people living in the rural areas where TV is not available. In addition, dozens of radio stations transmit across the country. Both private and public stations reach NWFP, and the impact of Taliban media propaganda on these channels is quite limited. However, mainstream media has been threatened in NWFP (notably in Swat and some localities of Mardan and Tank districts), and *fatwas* (religious edicts) have been issued demanding that television sets be destroyed.

The TTP and allied groups have an effective media and communications strategy using traditional and modern means of communication (both legal and illegal) as well as intimidation tactics designed to reduce the influence of mainstream media outlets. Militants operating in FATA have used night letters, pamphlets, CDs, DVDs, or mobile phone text messaging to gain attention and legitimacy. Baitullah Mehsud, chief of the Pakistani Taliban, used an interview with the US government-funded VOA's Pashto-language Deewa Radio to announce his threat of attacking the White House, which was well-publicized in US domestic media.

FM RADIO

The use of unlicensed FM transmitters to produce radio broadcasts is a favorite communications tool of the TTP. In some areas, illegal FM radio stations operate at frequencies reserved for government security forces, jeopardizing official communication links. At other times, illegal broadcasts have been used to weaken popular support for Pakistani military operations. For example, during a May 2009 operation in Malakand and Buner, in which the Pakistani government sought information from locals, the Taliban countered by broadcasting warnings against supporting the military. As a mark of protest against the military operations, the Taliban repeatedly demanded local politicians, security forces, and other government officials resign from their positions or prepare for a "jihad" directed against them.

These radio broadcasters, popularly known as "FM Mullahs," continuously transmit anti-American and anti-government sermons, calling democracy "un-Islamic" and those practicing it "infidels." In their fiery radio transmissions, militant preachers have also demanded that the non-Muslim minorities of Malakand pay *jizya* (Islamic protection tax) or face death. Additional warnings have been issued to local NGOs and musicians involved in what the broadcasters consider "un-Islamic" activities. Those defying the orders of the FM Mullahs have been killed, and details of their deaths were broadcast.

Officials in the Pakistan Electronic Media Regulation Authority (PEMRA, the country's media watchdog) estimate that there are 108 unlicensed FM radio stations in both FATA and NWFP. Independent observers believe the figures to be closer to 125-150 stations. Roughly 30 percent of these are functioning in NWFP, especially Swat, Dera Ismail Khan, Tank, Hangu, and Bannu. Some FM radio broadcasts from FATA can also be heard in adjacent NWFP districts like Peshawar and Kohat.

Setting up an unlicensed FM radio station in a mosque or madrassa is simple, requiring only a radiator-shaped transmitter, a basic amplifier, and a car-battery. These components are inexpensive and easily available in NWFP markets. According to local sources, an FM channel can cost $200 to $1,000, depending on its transmitter quality. PEMRA officials maintain that signals of most of the illegal FM channels work only within a 25-30 km range, but those with powerful FM transmitters have listeners as far as 50-60 km away. These radio channels can be received by any commercially available FM band receiver.

MAINSTREAM MEDIA IN NWFP

Popular Television Stations

Pakistan Television or PTV (state-controlled): Until recently, Pakistan Television was the only source of information. Its dramas, talk shows, comedies, and music programs are widely watched. *www.ptv.com*

Geo TV (private and liberal): One of the most popular TV stations, Geo TV has separate channels for news, entertainment, sports, and youth, and is accessible to about 30 percent of NWFP. *www.geo.tv*

ARY Digital (private and right of center/conservative): It provides separate channels for news and entertainment, reaching about 30 percent of NWFP. *www.arydigital.tv*

Express News TV (private and liberal): Considered among the most credible, it reaches about 30 percent of NWFP. *www.expressnews.tv*

AAJ TV (private and liberal): Among the most popular and progressive, it reaches about 30 percent of NWFP. *www.aaj.tv*

Dawn News TV (private): The first exclusively English-language news channel, Dawn News TV is considered progressive and liberal, reaching about 20 percent of NWFP. *www.dawn.com*

Samaa TV (private): A news channel that reaches about 25 percent of NWFP. *www.samaa.tv*

AVT Khyber (private and liberal): A Pashto-language news and entertainment channel popular in NWFP – also popular in some provinces of Afghanistan like Nangarhar, Kandahar, and even in Kabul. It is accessible in about 50 percent of NWFP. AVT Khyber's strength lies in the music program that attracts young viewers from across the world. Its phone-in programs such as *Sandaries Paighamoona* (Messages in Music), and "songs on demand" are very popular among young people. *www.khybernews.tv*

Popular Radio Channels

Pakistan Radio's Peshawar center (state-controlled) airs programs on social, political, cultural, medical, and religious issues, as well as dramas, comedy shows, and music. *Da Khyber Awaz* (Voice of Khyber), *Nawey Shar* (New Dawn), and *Khabre Atare* (Chit Chat), are popular programs.

Voice of America (VOA) airs a six-hour radio program of news and information in Pashto, Urdu, and English on FM, AM, shortwave, and the internet. It is broadcast across Pakistan, with a focus on the Pakistan-Afghanistan border, from 12 AM until 6 AM.

FM 101 (state-controlled) reaches listeners in Peshawar and Quetta, and airs programs in both Pashto and Urdu. Its primary audience is young listeners.

Radio Buraq broadcasts to Peshawar mostly in Urdu and partially in Pashto. Owned by a private company (the owner of the *Mashriq* group of newspapers), its style, format, and content target young listeners.

FM 102 Bannu, the state-run FM channel, broadcasts to the southern Bannu City that borders North Waziristan agency.

FM 94 Kohat broadcasts 12 hours daily directly from Radio Pakistan Islamabad. It airs information primarily on weather and sports as well as providing music and entertainment programs.

FM Lucky 88, a private FM channel created in 2004 in the southern city of Lakki Marwat, is owned by a local influential political family, the Saif Group.

Newspapers

About 5-7 percent of the people in NWFP urban areas read English-language newspapers, while 30-40 percent read Urdu-language newspapers (see Table 8).

Pashto-Language Newspapers:

Daily "Wahdat" **(Unity):** Launched in 1976, the paper initially was issued on a weekly basis but transitioned to daily distribution after the Soviet invasion of Afghanistan in 1979. It remains a popular source of information among the Afghans living in refugee camps in Pakistan.

Daily Hewad (**Country**): Launched in 1959, the four-page paper covers news, editorials, op-ed articles, and columns on the issues related to Pashtun social values, economic needs, and cultural and religious norms on both sides of the border in Afghanistan and Pakistan. In its editorials, the paper has mostly been advocating the unity of the Pashtuns on both sides of the Durand line.

Daily Khabroona (**News**): Its readers are drawn primarily from among the Afghan population living in refugee camps. Paper topics relate to issues of interest amongst the refugee population.

Table 7. Journals and Magazines

NAME	LANGUAGE	WEBSITE	FREQUENCY	NOTES
The Friday Times	English	www.thefridaytimes.com	weekly	A popular and progressive magazine
Herald	English	www.dawn.com/herald/	monthly	A respected magazine
Newsline	English	www.newsline.com.pk	monthly	A progressive and credible magazine
Akbar-e Jehan	Urdu	www.akhbar-e-jehan.com/home/index.php	weekly	Has wide circulation
Urdu Digest	Urdu	www.urdudigest.com.pk	monthly	One of the oldest and most influential magazines
Fact Urdu	Urdu	www.fact.com.pk/facturdu/fact.htm	monthly	Investigative magazine
Tarjuman ul Quran	Urdu	www.tarjumanulquran.org		A conservative and religious magazine, linked with *Jamaat-i-Islami*, a religious party

Table 8. Newspapers of NWFP

NAME	LANGUAGE	WEBSITE	NOTES
Dawn	English	*www.dawn.com*	Oldest and among the most popular and credible
The News	English	*www.thenews.com.pk*	Most widely read
Daily Times	English	*www.dailytimes.com.pk*	Progressive and liberal paper with limited circulation
The Nation	English	*www.nation.com.pk*	One of the oldest newspapers that is popular among right of centre audience
The Frontier Post	English	*www.frontierpost.com.pk*	Progressive newspaper published from Peshawar city and mostly read in NWFP and Quetta
The Statesman	English	*www.statesman.com.pk*	Published from Peshawar and is mostly read in the area
Jang	Urdu	*www.jang.com.pk*	Most widely read newspaper, has the same owners as The News and GEO TV
Nawa-i Waqt	Urdu	*www.nawaiwaqt.com.pk*	Leading conservative newspaper; also owns The Nation
Khabrain	Urdu	*www.khabrain.com*	
Ausaf	Urdu	*www.dailyausaf.com*	Has a conservative slant
Express	Urdu	*www.express.com.pk*	Popular paper
Mashriq	Urdu	*www.dailymashriq.com.pk*	Popular paper
Daily "Wahdat" (Unity)	Pashto	none	Popular among Afghans
Daily Hewad (Country)	Pashto	none	
Daily Khabroona (News)	Pashto	none	Focuses on refugee issues

With an increase in violence towards Pakistani security forces and government targets, Islamabad has ceased its long-standing disinterest in challenging Islamic militants.

PHOTO BY ANTHONY MAW

Appendix

FURTHER READING AND SOURCES

Useful Links

- The Government of NWFP, *www.nwfp.gov.pk*
- Official Malakand website, *www.malakand.8m.com/index.html*
- Mardan, *www.mardan.com*
- Batagram, *www.unjlc.org/23003/pakistan/infosheets/snapshots/batagram_region/view*
- Palas Valley (around Kohistan District), *www.palasvalley.org*
- Lakki Marwat, *www.khyber.org/pashtoplaces/lakkimarwat2.shtml & www.ugood.org/reports/Report%20on%20Lakki%20Marwat.pdf*
- Buner, *www.buner.gov.pk*
- Chitral Today, *www.chitraltoday.com*
- Sarhad Chamber of Commerce, *www.scci.org.pk*
- NWFP Text book board, *www.nwfptbb.gov.pk/mission.html*
- Peshawar, *www.khyber.org/places/2007/TheWalledCity.shtml*

- Swat, *www.valleyswat.net*

- Report of Geological Survey of Pakistan (including NWFP area), *www.gsp.gov.pk/parvezmusharraf_071206.pdf*

- NWFP planning reform, *www.nwfpfinance.gov.pk/wpp_Buget_analysis.php*

Reports & Articles

- Joshua T. White, "Pakistan's Islamist Frontier." Center on Faith & International Affairs, 2008.

- C. Christine Fair, "The Madrassah Challenge: Militancy and Religious Education in Pakistan," Washington, D.C.: United States Institute of Peace Press, 2008.

- *International Crisis Group*, "Pakistan's Tribal Areas: Appeasing the Militants," Asia Report 125, 11 (December 2006).

- Hassan Abbas, "From FATA to NWFP: The Taliban Spread Their Grip in Pakistan," *CTC Sentinel*, Volume 1, Issue 10, pages 3-5, September 2008.

- Barnett R. Rubin and Abubakar Siddique, "Resolving the Pakistan-Afghanistan Stalemate," *United States Institute of Peace*, Special Report, October 2006.

- Mukhtar A. Khan, "The FM Mullahs and Taliban's Propaganda War in Pakistan," The Jamestown Foundation, *Terrorism Monitor*; Volume 7, Issue 14; May 26, 2009.

Books

- Hassan Abbas, *Pakistan's Drift into Extremism: Allah, the Army and America's War on Terror,* New York: M E Sharpe, 2005.

- Peter Bergen, *The Osama bin Laden I know: An Oral History of al Qaeda Leader*, New York: Free Press, 2006.

- Steve Cohen, *The Idea of Pakistan*, Washington, D.C.: Brookings, 2004.

- Steve Coll. *Ghost Wars,* New York: Penguin, 2004.

- Greg Mortenson and David Oliver Relin, *Three Cups of Tea: One Man's Mission to Promote Peace...One School at a Time,* New York: Penguin, 2007.

- Jules Stewart, *The Savage Border: The Story of the North-West Frontier,* South Carolina: The History Press, 2007.

- George Crile, *Charlie Wilson's War: The Extraordinary Story of the Largest Covert Operation in History,* Atlantic Monthly Press, 2003.

- Ahmed Rashid, *Descent Into Chaos*, London: Viking, 2008.

www.ingramcontent.com/pod-product-compliance
Lightning Source LLC
Chambersburg PA
CBHW040128270326
41927CB00001B/32